Team BLOOM's

WE LOVE
DRIED FLOWERS

Handmade wreaths,
room decorations
& bouquets

Wildflower.Media

CONTENTS

BASICS

What exactly are dried flowers? And what needs to be considered when dealing with them? In this chapter, you will learn everything you need to know about permanent and dried flowers - from tips and tricks on collecting and harvesting the right plants through the various drying techniques and the suitable aids and tools for processing.

WHAT ARE DRIED FLOWERS?

Real dried flowers naturally form in the garden from already dry flower parts – for example, everlasting flowers or *Hydrangea*. These are also easy to grow and use from your own garden.

Dutch dried flowers are those that are produced and marketed in large quantities by Dutch and other companies. The product range extends from roses to plant materials, from statice to *Dahlia*, and includes almost 200 types of dried flowers and plants. Many of these products can be grown or collected yourself.

Dry exotic species come from distant countries. They are the parts of plants that are already naturally drying, such as nut fruit shells and palms, but also technically dried parts such as some *Protea*. You have to buy these materials online, from a wholesaler or, perhaps, a florist. As a rule, self-collected items are not allowed to be exported and not imported to the United States. To be sure, there are many species protected by international agreements as well as corresponding national laws to be observed.

Other dry materials come from pine cones, tree fungi and pieces of bark. You can also use dried fruits such as nuts and the like that come from native species in the United States and elsewhere.

Bushy yate, Gum tree
(*Eucalyptus lehmannii*)

Rose (*Rosa* cultivar)

Palmyra palm
(*Borassus flabellifer*)

WHAT & HOW TO COLLECT MATERIALS

In your own garden, harvesting and collecting is largely problem free and allowed to a large extent, unless strictly protected species grow there. Protected or dangerous species must not be harvested anywhere. This is also the case in protected areas like state and federal parks, preserves and other areas. Avoid collecting all types and parts of plants where prohibited. In all other cases, property rights may have to be observed. Where collection is allowed, take care not to damage the entire inventory on site. Above all, be aware that annual plants reproduce only through seeds, to propogate their species. Always leave some behind for the next growing season. Being thoughtful while collecting is good for you, the environment and for sustainability.

COLLECT ING AND HARVESTING IN NATURE OR IN THE GARDEN:

Eulalia, Chinese silver grass (*Miscanthus sinensis*) »inflorescence, stalks and leaves
Dahlia (*Dahlia*) »flowers
Lavender (*Lavandula angustifolia*) »fragrant inflorescence
Fennel (*Foeniculum vulgare*) »branched inflorescence
Fern-leaf yarrow (*Achillea filipendulina*) »branched inflorescence
Hortensia (*Hydrangea*) »panicle-shaped inflorescence
Canary grass (*Phalaris canariensis*) »spike inflorescence, stalks and leaves
Globe thistle (*Echinops ritro*) »globular fruit cluster
Eryngo, Sea holly (*Eryngium*) »thistle-like infructescence
Needle palm (*Rhapidophyllum hystrix*) »leaves
Purple-flowered onion (*Allium atropurpureum*) »inflorescence
Giant onion (*Allium giganteum*) »spherical inflorescence
Rabbit-tail grass (*Lagurus ovatus*) »spike inflorescence, stalks and leaves
Pincushion flower (*Scabiosa atropurpurea*) »branched inflorescence
Baby's breath (*Gypsophila paniculata*) »branched inflorescence
Silver dollar (*Lunaria annua*) »fruit partitions of the pods

Baby's breath
(*Gypsophila paniculata*)

Hortensia (*Hydrangea*)

9

COLLECTING AND HARVESTING IN NATURE OR IN THE GARDEN:
Sunflower (*Helianthus annuus*) »flower heads and roots
Strawflower, Everlasting (*Helipterum roseum*) »flowers and leaves
Butcher's broom (*Ruscus aculeatus*) »short shoots
Stars-of-Persia (*Allium christophii*) »spherical inflorescence
Starflower scabious, Starflower pincushion (*Scabiosa stellata*) »spherical fruit cluster
Statice, Sea lavender (*Limonium spp.*) »flowers and leaves
Everlasting daisy, Paper daisy, Strawflower (*Xerochrysum bracteatum*) »cup-shaped inflorescence
Billy button, Drumstick (*Pycnosorus globosus*, formerly *Craspedia globosa*) »spherical inflorescence
Virgin's bower (*Clematis spp.*) »fluffy fruit clusters, flexible tendrils
Indian teasel, Fuller's teasel (*Dipsacus sativus*) »thistle-like infructescence
Wild teasel, Common teasel (*Dipsacus fullonum*) »thistle-like fruit cluster
Quaking grass (*Briza media*) »spike inflorescence, stalks and leaves

EXOTIC DRIED FLOWERS:
(Collecting as souvenirs and imports are usually prohibited)
Cape strawflower, Cape everlasting (*Phaenocoma prolifera*) »flowers
Cotton (*Gossypium herbaceum*) »open-capsule fruit
Hemp palm, Chinese windmill palm (*Trachycarpus fortunei*) »leaves
Eucalypt, Gum tree (*Eucalyptus spp.*) »leaves, inflorescence and fruits
Sago palm, Japanese sago palm, Japanese fern palm (*Cycas revoluta*) »leaves
Coral fern, Umbrella fern (*Gleichenia microphylla*) »leaves
Palmyra palm (*Borassus flabellifer*) »leaves
Pampas grass (*Cortaderia selloana*) »inflorescence, stalks and leaves
Rice flower (*Ozothamnus diosmifolius*) »inflorescence
Silver wattle, Mimosa (*Acacia dealbata*) »racemose inflorescence
Silver tree (*Leucadendron argenteum, L. sabulosum*) »
   cone-like inflorescence remnant
Protea, Sugar bush (*Protea spp.*) »flowers and leaves
Bird's-nest banksia (*Banksia baxteri*) »oval inflorescence
Bird-of-paradise (*Strelitzia reginae*) »flowers and leaves
Air plant (*Tillandsia spp.*) »whole plant or individual leaves
Sugar cane blooms (*Saccharum officinarum*) »inflorescence,
   culms and leaves

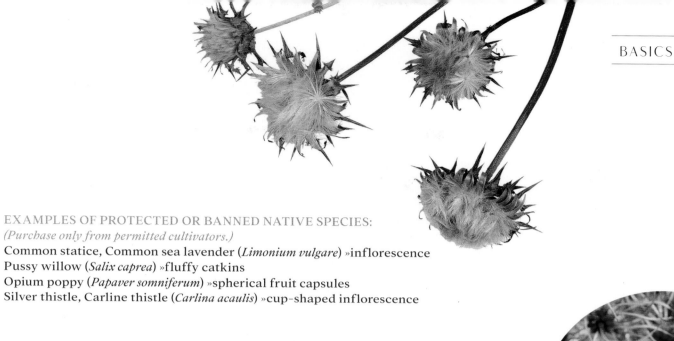

EXAMPLES OF PROTECTED OR BANNED NATIVE SPECIES:
(Purchase only from permitted cultivators.)
Common statice, Common sea lavender (*Limonium vulgare*) »inflorescence
Pussy willow (*Salix caprea*) »fluffy catkins
Opium poppy (*Papaver somniferum*) »spherical fruit capsules
Silver thistle, Carline thistle (*Carlina acaulis*) »cup-shaped inflorescence

HOW IS IT HARVESTED?
The right degree of maturity is fairly decisive, but that of one species can
be different from other species. In general, you will harvest flowers
that are fully developed. But there are exceptions, such as the
strawflower, which is cut just before the flower opening.
It develops as it dries into a fully blossomed state. It also
makes sense to harvest on dry, sunny days, as soon as
there is no more dew or rain on the parts of the plant.

Clematis spp.

Indian teasel (*Dipsacus sativus*)

Statice, Sea lavender
(*Limonium latifolium*)

11

WHICH DRYING TECHNIQUES ARE BEST?

In general, drying flowers is about the gentlest way to withdraw moisture contained in plants and flowers while trying to preserve the most color in the blooms, leaves and stems. A natural change in color, for example, from green grass to dull green hay or yellowish straw, can be hard to avoid. Although this is possible with professional drying, for example, by freeze-drying, it is not feasible for those working at home or in flower shops. If you want professional results, you'll often times have to buy professionally dried botanicals. However, you can try the following methods yourself. Experimenting with different materials and drying methods can often give you great results at a fraction of the cost.

AIR DRYING:

This technique is carried out in a dry and airy place, which is also dark because of the color retention, at room temperature. It is best to hang the plant parts upside down, in small bundles, so that the stems remain largely straight. There should be a maximum of ten stems per bunch so that good ventilation can prevent mold growth. Rubber bands, as binders, are beneficial because they compensate for the volume shrinkage of the stems during drying and nothing will fall out of the bundle.
Very strong stems can also be dried standing in a container and individual leaves lying on a wire mesh.

WARM AIR DRYING:

Drying is relatively quick in an oven but also in a small room with a hot fan. Using a hot fan uses the method outlined above. In the oven, on the other hand, individual leaves and petals or flowers with short stems are dried. This is done either on the baking rack or a baking sheet covered with clean sand. First, heat your oven to it's lowest setting, or about 100° F. Then distribute the florals to be dried with sufficient space between them, and leave them in the oven for varying lengths of time, depending on their consistency. Petals are ready in about thirty minutes while whole stems and stronger materials take several hours. Often, experimentation is needed to obtain best results.

DRYING WITH DESICCANTS:

Dry salt; borax (sodium borate/tetraborate) or a laundry detergent like 20 Mule Team Borax; or silica gel can be used for this technique. The plants and flowers must be in a closed container and must be completely surrounded by the respective desiccant. The more sensitive the material, the more carefully the drying agent has to be poured in or sprinkled around it. In general, the more fine-grained the desiccant, the better it can work. After about a week, the drying process should be complete, and the removal is again carried out very carefully. While salt and laundry detergent can be used only once, silica gel can be regenerated in the oven at 250° F to 300° F and is, therefore, reusable. Colored silica gel indicates the state of loading with water, but has been classified as harmful for some time, especially the dust.

DRYING AND PRESSING WITH A PLANT PRESS OR DRYING BOOK:

This variant works only with individual petals or very delicate plant parts. You need two layers of paper, with the leaves or flowers placed between them. Then these layers are placed into a thick book, and the book is closed, and the layers are weighted with another book or several books. Alternatively, appropriately designed plant presses are available for this purpose. Pressing or weighting ensures good contact between the plant part and the paper, so that the dehydration works optimally. It also serves to maintain the shape of the plant materials during the drying process. Depending on the material, this process takes up to three weeks. It is advisable to carefully replace the paper with new dry layers from time to time, particularly in high-humidity environments.

HOW DO I PROPERLY DEAL WITH DRIED FLOWERS?

In general, dried flowers should not be exposed to direct sunlight so that they keep their color for as long as possible. Too high of a humidity level is also unfavorable because mold can build up in the process. Because of the risk of breakage, delicate, sensitive dried flowers should not be touched, if possible, so avoid moving or adjusting them, if possible. You can also protect individual dry florals by sealing them with hairspray, clear lacquer or a special sealing spray for dried flowers. Always maintain a sufficient distance while spraying, and avoid spraying too thick. If you are careful, you can enjoy your dried floral creation for many years to come.

BEST
TIPS & TOOLS

If you want to design and decorate individually with dried flowers, you'll need some tips and the proper tools. Here is an overview of the most important helpers.

BEST TIPS:

In addition to tying a bouquet of dried flowers, there are many other shaping and positioning techniques. The following tools offer all the best possibilities.

· Paddle or spool wire (binding wire)
· Paper-covered wire
· Lengths of enameled wire
· Rebar tie wires
· Wire forms (wreaths, etc.)
· Wire mesh (chicken wire, rabbit-cage wire)
· Dried floral foam products
  (brick, ball, sheet, cone, etc.)
· Various adhesives
  (hot glue, liquid floral adhesive, craft glue)
· Duct tape

THE RIGHT TOOLS:

In general, any tool that enables meaningful use of the material is helpful. The following items are most useful and highly recommended.

· Hot glue gun
· Combination pliers
· Knife
· Snips or pruners
· Scissors
· Staple gun
· Cordless screwdriver
· Drill and bits
· Hammer
· Rebar tie wire wisting tool

WE LOVE
TABLE FLOWERS

When talking about dried flowers, table decorations should not be missed. The following chapter offers various do-it-yourself projects. But permanent florals are also real eye-catchers in the form of wreaths and miniature trees sideboards and windowsills.

BOHO PLACE CARDS

Simple but effective! Whether for a casual garden party or a lavish wedding party, the quickly made place card conjures a smile on the faces of guests at every occasion.

HOW TO DO IT:

A dried palmyra palm leaf serves as the background for your design. Next, a *Eucalyptus* sprig with the guest's name on the leaf is placed on the palm leaf, together with a cotton blossom. To finish the design, tie it all together with paper-covered wire.

DRIED BOTANICALS:
· Palmyra palm
· *Eucalyptus*
· Cotton

MATERIALS & TOOLS:
· Paper-covered wire
· Felt pen

19

LUSH STAGING

With needle palm, Chinese silver grass and rice flower, this stylish bouquet looks particularly expansive and attracts everyone's attention in the room. Place it into a bulbous glass vase to perfectly fit the scene.

HOW TO DO IT:

The flowers are made into a lush bouquet with the help of a binding tie of raffia. Place the flowers in the middle, and design the edge with needle palm and rice flower. Let the Chinese silver grass protrude airily from the arrangement. Wire in shorter botanical materials, and place into the vase.

DRIED BOTANICALS:
· *Protea*
· *Hydrangea*
· Strawflowers/
  Everlastings
· Statice, Sea lavender
· Starflower scabious
· Rice flower
· *Strelitzia*
· *Lunaria*
· Wild teasels
· Needle palm
· Chinese silver grass

MATERIALS & TOOLS:
· Vase
· Raffia
· Wire

GARDEN TO GO

A mini terrarium with dried flowers and fruit bunches not only looks great on the table at home or at a party but also serves as a souvenir for family and friends.

HOW TO DO IT:
Combine poppy seed capsules with coral fern, or perhaps you prefer *Protea* with *Scabiosa*? There are no limits to your imagination: Put your favorite combination together, and arrange them in a canning jar or candy jar. Then cut a transparent paper lid to size, place it on top and secure it with a rubber band. Cover the rubber band with paper-covered wire. Put a wood skewer through the paper-covered wire, and if desired, add a label printed on a piece of kraft paper.

DRIED BOTANICALS:
· *Protea*
· Sunflowers
· *Scabiosa*
· Strawflowers/
  Everlastings
· Cape everlastings
· Rice flower
· Poppy seed capsules
· Needle palm
· Coral fern

MATERIALS & TOOLS:
· Glass jars
· Transparent paper
· Wrapping paper
· Wooden skewers
· Rubber bands
· Paper-covered wire
· Pen or printer
· Scissors

23

FLOWER BALLS IN PASTELS

A delicate feast for the eyes! Instead of sweet desserts on a plate, place flower balls on your cake plate. For this design, we use everlasting dried flowers in various pastel hues.

HOW TO DO IT:
Sort the everlasting dried flowers by color, and use pins to affix each of them on the different sized dry-floral-foam spheres. Then place them on a cake plate. A round lace doily creates an additional subtle accent.

DRIED BOTANICALS:
· Strawflowers/Everlastings in two colors

MATERIALS & TOOLS:
· Two dry-floral-foam spheres of different sizes
· Cake platter
· Knitted lace doily
· Pins

WIRY MINI TREE

A bonsai tree with a difference! This little tree, with a wire trunk and a dried flower crown, is not only easy to care for but also looks great whether on a table, a windowsill or a sideboard.

HOW TO DO IT:
Be sure the stone you use is heavy enough to prevent the tree from tipping over. Once you have a suitable stone, drill a hole in it.

(1) Insert four or five lengths of wire, twist them together to form a tree trunk and bend several of them horizontally to form branches. Thin-gauge paddle or spool wire can now be worked into a dense web atop the wire branches.

(2) Once the wire top ball has been formed, the flowers can simply be tucked in (and glued, if you want it to be more secure).

DRIED BOTANICALS:
· Rice flower
· Strawflowers/
  Everlatings
· *Hydrangea*
· Starflower scabious
· Chinese silver grass

MATERIALS
& TOOLS:
· Stone
· Wire
· Paddle or spool wire
· Drill
· Wire cutters

WREATH DOUBLE TAKE

When hung on a bare branch, two kinds of wreaths come out big. A nice contrast is created when one is kept in a simple white and green while the other uses rich colors.

HOW TO DO IT:

Wire the plants and flowers in their respective combinations, with the help of decorative wire. Then tie or wire the flowers to the wire rings. Put the branch into a vase, to hold it vertically and provide a base of support. Attach a piece of string to each of the wreaths, and knot them to the branch.

DRIED BOTANICALS:
White wreath:
· Strawflowers/
  Everlastings
· *Clematis*
· Statice/Sea lavender
· *Eucalyptus*
· Ravenna grass
· Canary grass

Orange wreath:
· Strawflowers/
  Everlastings
· *Hydrangea*
· Statice/Sea lavender
· *Eucalyptus*
· Ravenna grass
· Deciduous branch

MATERIALS & TOOLS:
· Two wire wreath
  rings
· Decorative wire
· Vase
· String/Twine

29

ENCHANTING BOUQUET

With a delicate interplay of dried flowers in pastel hues and various airy grasses, this design score points with your guests. The compactly bound bouquet exudes a permanent summer mood.

HOW TO DO IT:

First wire on short florals such as fruited clusters. Then gather the flowers, fruited clusters and grasses, and arrange them to form a round bouquet. Secure with binding wire or twine. Place the bouquet at an angle in a wide vase.

DRIED BOTANICALS:
- Strawflowers/ Everlastings
- Cape everlastings
- *Protea*
- *Hydrangea*
- Poppy seed capsules
- Wild teasels
- Bird's-nest *Banksia*
- Pampas grass
- Quaking grass

MATERIALS & TOOLS:
- Vase
- Binding wire or twine
- Wire

31

BACK TO THE ROOTS

Decorative sunflower roots play a key role in this ensemble for the tall inflorescences of the purple-flowered *Allium*. They take turns on a wood tray with flower-filled vases.

HOW TO DO IT:
The tall *Allium* inflorescences are given stability in the vases by putting them together with coral fern and using paper-covered wire tied to woody sunflower stalks with roots. Fill the vases with the remaining botanicals, and arrange them alternately with the *Allium* ensembles on a tray.

DRIED BOTANICALS:
· Purple-flowered
    Allium
· *Protea*
· Rice flower
· Needle palm
· Coral fern
· Feather reed grass
· Sunflower stems
    with roots

**MATERIALS
& TOOLS:**
· Small vases
· Tray
· Cord
· Wire

BEHIND GLASS

Plants and flowers cast in plaster work under glass cloches make dry florals like valuable exhibits — and no dust is guaranteed! Simply add to your windowsill or table for full effect.

HOW TO DO IT:
Cut pieces of dry-floral foam so they fit under the glass cloches. Shorten flowers and grasses, if necessary, and arrange them into the foam pieces. Then mix plaster according to the package instructions, pour it over the floral foam and allow to dry. Place the final designs on plates, under glass cloches.

DRIED BOTANICALS:
· Strawflowers/Everlastings
· Rabbit-tail grass

MATERIALS & TOOLS:
· Two cloches in different
  sizes, with plates
· Dry-floral foam
· Plaster of Paris
· Bucket
· Wood stick for stirring
· Knife

FROM A MOLDING

A picture of a wreath of flowers is created in no time by casting the piece of art in plaster. A great eye-catcher on a table, which can alternatively decorate a wall.

HOW TO DO IT:
Work the dry florals into a floral-foam wreath form. Use wood boards and screws to make a square form. Mix the plaster according to the instructions on the package, and pour it into the wood mold so that the bottom is covered. Now put the flower wreath in, fill the mold again with plaster and let it dry. Finally, remove the wood form.

DRIED BOTANICALS:
· *Scabiosa*
· Strawflowers/ Everlastings
· Japanese chaff flowers
· Wild teasels
· Rabbit-tail grass
· Quaking grass

MATERIALS & TOOLS:
· Dry-floral-foam wreath
· Plaster of Paris
· Bucket
· Wood stick for stirring
· Four wood boards of equal length
· Square wood board for the background
· Screws
· Screwdriver

HIGH DESIGN

This impressive standing bouquet rises up. Guinea fowl feathers and rice flower create a gentle, soft contrast to the palm leaves and ferns. That certain something is created by adding poppy seed capsules.

HOW TO DO IT:

First, the guinea fowl feathers are wired with binding wire and then tied together with the florals to form an upward-pointing bouquet. Tie the bouquet with raffia. Flowers and poppy seed capsules in the middle should be half enclosed by higher florals. Place into a wide bowl.

DRIED BOTANICALS:
· Statice/Sea lavender
· Montbretia
· *Clematis*
· Rice flower
· Poppy seed capsules
· Palmyra palm
· Sago palm
· *Euclayptus*
· Millet
· Meadow grasses

MATERIALS & TOOLS:
· Bowl
· Guinea fowl feathers
· Raffia
· Binding wire

SHINING HIGHLIGHT

In a cake pan from a flea market, a wreath with everlasting dried flowers and textiles is especially good in a kitchen. A coordinating candle puts it all in the right light.

HOW TO DO IT:

Cover a straw wreath outside and inside with scraps of wool, and place it in a cake pan. Adhere everlasting dried flowers onto the wreath using pins or hot glue. Insert a fringed ribbon in the transition area between the flowers and the knitted fabric. Finally, set a suitable candle in the center of the wreath, and put everything on a wood plate.

DRIED BOTANICALS:
· Strawflowers/Everlastings

MATERIALS & TOOLS:
· Straw wreath
· Wool fabric remnants
· Fringed ribbon
· Candle
· Wood plate
· Cake pan
· Hot glue or pins

41

WE LOVE WALL DECORATIONS

In trendy flower hoops and wreaths as well as stylish 3D pictures
in picture or embroidery frames, dried botanicals look great on walls.
Regardless of whether the design is expertly wrapped, wound, wired,
picked or glued, you'll find success with the following ideas.

STYLISH WREATH

This imposing wreath is an absolute eye-catcher on a wall!
Plus, it doesn't take much to create this amazing impact.
You need only dried flowers, grasses, a metal wreath
ring and some wire.

HOW TO DO IT:

Place the florals on the wire ring as you like.
While doing so, it is best to be narrower
toward the top and more lush toward the
bottom, and fix the materials with binding
wire. For shorter materials, you may want
to create small bundles, wired together,
and then wire the bundles to wire base.

DRIED BOTANICALS:

· *Hydrangea*
· Strawflowers/Everlastings
· *Gypsophila*
· Globe thistles
· *Eucalyptus*
· Butcher's broom
· Palmyra palm
· Pampas grass
· Bleached ornamental grass

MATERIALS & TOOLS:

· Wire wreath ring
· Binding wire
· Wire

BOHO FLOWER HOOP

You are guaranteed to be right on trend using this stylish flower hoop in which the wire ring is part of the decoration. Beautiful *Eucalyptus* plays the main role, while *Banksia* and *Protea* provide an exotic note.

HOW TO DO IT:

This floral arrangement boasts an asymmetrical design with the help of a decorative wire ring. Decorate the wire ring so that about half of it remains visible. Affix the botanicals with hot glue and wire. Finally, attach a ribbon cord to hang it, and knot a torn strip of fabric as an decorative accent from the top.

DRIED BOTANICALS:
· Strawflowers/
  Everlastings
· *Banksia*
· *Protea*
· Wild teasels
· Silver tree
· *Eucalyptus*
· Canary grass
· Pampas grass

MATERIALS & TOOLS:
· Gold wire ring
· Torn strip of fabric
· Tape
· Decorative wire
· Hot glue

FLOWERS IN AN EMBROIDERY HOOP

An embroidery frame creates the perfect backdrop for the staging of sea lavender and *Gypsophila*. With a little hot glue, the botanical materials are very quickly attached to the nettle fabric background in the shape of a wreath.

HOW TO DO IT:
Cut the nettle fabric to size, and insert it into the embroidery hoop, stretching the fabric tight. Then cut the stems from the dried flowers, and using hot glue, attach the flowers to the fabric in the shape of a wreath.

DRIED BOTANICALS:
· Statice/Sea lavender
· *Gypsophila*
· Bleached butcher's broom
· Red pepper berries
· Silver tree
· Ornamental grass

MATERIALS & TOOLS:
· Embroidery hoop
· Nettle fabric
· Hot glue
· Scissors

RUSTIC VINES

If you have to go fast: A ready-made vine wreath from the florist supply store is the perfect base for this wall wreath, loosely decorated with *Clematis*, dry flowers and fruit bunches.

HOW TO DO IT:
Cover the vine wreath wildly with *Clematis* vines so that there are also some tendrils to the sides. The remaining botanicals can be clipped and then wired or glued in loosely.

DRIED BOTANICALS:
· Strawflowers/Everlastings
· Panicle *Hydrangea*
· Tansies
· Indian teasels
· *Lunaria*
· *Clematis*
· Vine wreath

MATERIALS & TOOLS:
· Wire
· Hot Glue

DRIED FLOWER FRAME

The highlight of this mural is that the dried botanicals concentrate on one corner of the black frame and casually protrude from it. A simple plastic-foam ball creates the floral design base.

HOW TO DO IT:
(1) Cut the plastic-foam ball in half with a long knife.
(2) Secure one of the hemispheres (half spheres) in a lower corner of the empty picture frame, flat side down, using waterproof florist tape or hot glue, or both.
(3) Arrange the dried botanicals, with the help of wire, if needed, all around the plastic-foam hemisphere to create your design.

DRIED BOTANICALS:
· Giant *Allium*
· Bird's-nest *Banksia*
· *Tillandsia*
· Coral fern
· Chinese hemp palm
· Palmyra palm
· Pampas grass
· *Agave* leaves
· *Strelitzia* leaves

MATERIALS & TOOLS:
· Picture frame
· Plastic-foam ball
· Duct tape
· Wire
· Knife
· Scissors

DRAMATIC IN ROSÉ

Dry doesn't mean colorless! This wreath boasts pink flowers of cape immortelles, strawflowers and sea lavender. When hung on a suitable frame, a modern still-life is created.

HOW TO DO IT:

Attach all botanical materials onto the wire ring with binding wire, leaving a section of the ring visible. Place materials narrowly at both ends, and widen the design in the middle. Glue in the leaves. By the way: Wire rings come in textured and smooth. A textured ring is recommended here because it is easier to grip and helps prevent the botanicals from slipping.

DRIED BOTANICALS:
· Cape immortelles/
  Cape everlastings
· Strawflowers/Everlastings
· Statice/Sea lavender
· *Hydrangea*
· Rice flower
· Silver ragwort
· Canary grass

MATERIALS & TOOLS:
· Textured wire ring
· Binding wire
· Hot glue

DELICATE HUES

This wall wreath exudes a touch of magic in restrained off-white and natural tones. Fluffy pussy willow, silver leaf and rice flower ensure lightness.

HOW TO DO IT:

(1) Create a wreath of hop bines, binding the stems together with rebar tie wire and using a rebar tie wire twisting tool. Bend the wire around the branches and then hook both eyelets onto the twisting tool's hook. Pull on the handle of the tool while twisting, firmly holding the vines at the binding point.

(2) Hot-glue the dried botanical materials onto the hop-bines wreath base. There should be many crossings of the stems, tendrils and stalks, to create a loose look.

DRIED BOTANICALS:

· Strawflowers/Everlastings
· Rice flower
· Pussy willow
· *Lunaria*
· Hop Bines
· Chinese silver grass
· Quaking grass

MATERIALS & TOOLS:

· Rebar tie wires
· Rebar tie wire twisting tool
· Hot glue

REFINED DESIGN

Clematis vines are used to create the basic framework of this wreath, which can be easily adapted to the desired loop shape. Yarrow, palm leaves and cotton are arranged asymmetrically though it.

HOW TO DO IT:

Wind the *Clematis* vines to form a wreath. Let the vines flow out at the bottom so that a kind of tail is formed. Secure the vines with binding wire. Wire or hot-glue the dried botanicals onto the right side of the vine wreath.

DRIED BOTANICALS:

· Strawflowers/Everlastings
· *Hydrangea*
· Fern-leaf yarrow
· *Lunaria*
· Cotton
· Indian teasels
· Palmyra palm
· *Clematis* vine

MATERIALS & TOOLS:

· Binding wire
· Hot glue

DRIED FLOWERS IN 3D

This floral stand features *Tillandsia*, fern and palm leaves designed on a decorative metal frame that provides the right shape and creates an exotic flair in a home.

HOW TO DO IT:
Use waterproof florist tape to adhere the dry-floral foam in one of the lower corners of the metal frame. Then arrange the botanical materials into the foam base. A metal rod can serve as a support for the taller botanicals.

DRIED BOTANICALS:
· Stars-of-Persia *Allium*
· Bird's-nest *Banksia*
· *Tillandsia*
· Sago palm
· Palmyra palm
· *Strelitzia* leaves

MATERIALS & TOOLS:
· Metal frame/stand
· Dry-floral foam
· Duct tape
· Scissors

61

COUNTRY FLAIR

Not only do billy buttons and everlastings provide color to this wall wreath but wired tufts of scrap fabric also catch the eye. Small bundles of straw exude country home chic.

HOW TO DO IT:
Cut scraps of fabric, roll them into tufts and wire them onto a straw wreath form. Create bundles of straw, and affix them to the wreath with pink decorative wire. Form short-stemmed bundles strawflowers/ everlastings and billy buttons, wiring the stems together. Hot-glue the bundles, as well as individual flowers, onto the straw wreath form. Attach a loop of sisal rope to the wreath, for hanging.

DRIED BOTANICALS:
· Strawflowers/Everlastings
· Billy buttons/Drumsticks
· Lavender
· Straw

MATERIALS & TOOLS:
· Straw wreath
· Scraps of fabric
· Sisal rope
· Pink decorative wire
· Wire
· Hot glue
· Scissors

GOLDEN WHEAT WREATH

A circular mural made of dried wheat, flowers, leaves and fruit stalks can easily be designed by beginners and is more of an excercise in diligence - sticking, sticking, sticking ...

HOW TO DO IT:

(1) Cut out a circle from sturdy cardboard. Hot-glue a wire hook to the backside of the cardboard, and glue another smaller piece of cardboard to overlap the ends of the wire hook. (2) Hot-glue short-stemmed bundles of wheat and Chinese silver grass onto the surface of the cardboard disk, radiating outward, starting around the outer edges of the disk and working toward the center, where you will place the other botanical materials.

DRIED BOTANICALS:
· Fern-leaf yarrow
· Billy buttons/
  Drumsticks
· *Hydrangea*
· Silver thistles/
  Carline thistles
· Starflower scabious
· Sugar-cane blooms
· Chinese silver grass
· *Strelitzia* leaves
· Wheat

MATERIALS & TOOLS:
· Cardboard
· Hot glue
· Wire
· Scissors

WE LOVE ROOM DÉCOR

Sometimes more is just more! For those who love a big showstopping design and have enough space at home, you can create something really special with dried and permanent flowers. This chapter offers spectacular ideas – from an innovative room divider to the imposing XXL standing bouquet to ground pots with dried flowers and plants.

IMPOSING COMPOSITION

Vessel in a vessel: A loose-weave wicker basket simply goes over the container and harmonizes perfectly with various dried botanicals such as pampas grass, stars-of-Persia *Allium* and palmyra palm.

HOW TO DO IT:
Gather all the botanical materials together, and tie them with raffia, creating a large bouquet. The notable feature here is the varying heights of the individual florals. Place the bouquet into a suitable container, and set that container into a wicker basket.

DRIED BOTANICALS:
· *Hydrangea*
· Rice flower
· Starflower scabious
· Stars-of-Persia *Allium*
· Giant hogweed
· Sago palm
· Palmyra palm
· Pampas grass

MATERIALS & TOOLS:
· Binding wire
· Container
· Wicker basket

Attention! The sap of the fresh giant hogweed is highly toxic! So don't pick the plant yourself; instead, seek a professionnally dried specimen at your favorite florist supply house.

69

EXTRA-LARGE STANDING BOUQUET

Every bouquet doesn't have to sit on a table or a sideboard to find its place. With the help of some wood sticks, you can create this gigantic standing bouquet, which is guaranteed to become the focus of a living space.

HOW TO DO IT:

All dried botanical materials are bundled and bound into a lush standing bouquet. Using the Dutch spiral method for hand-tying bouquets, a firm footing can be achieved. Simply trim stem ends to form a flat bottom so the bouquet will stand upright. Insert wood dowels for stability, if necessary. Place the final design into a decorative concrete bowl.

DRIED BOTANICALS:
· *Strelitzia* leaves
· Strawflowers/ Everlastings
· *Hydrangea*
· Billy buttons/ Drumsticks
· *Clematis*
· Fennel
· *Lunaria*
· Wild teasels
· Retama shrub
· Sago palm
· Chinese silver grass
· Pampas grass

MATERIALS & TOOLS:
· Wide concrete bowl
· Binding wire or raffia
· Wood dowels

71

A NATURAL ROOM DIVIDER

If you have a lot of space at home – and a little skill – you can create an impressive decorative object from dried botanicals that can be used as a room divider.

HOW TO DO IT:

Paint the wood beam base with white paint, and let dry. Then drill several holes into the top edge of the beam, and insert the stems of the botanical materials into the holes. If desired, secure the stems in the holes with hot glue.

DRIED BOTANICALS:
· Giant *Allium*
· Giant hogweed
· Wild teasels
· *Eucalyptus*
· Sago palm
· Palmyra palm
· Pampas grass

MATERIALS & TOOLS:
· Wood beam
· White paint
· Paint brush
· Drill
· Hot glue

CONCRETE POTTED PLANTS

Tall botanicals with strong stems, such as sunflowers, Chinese silver grass and Indian teasels, are an eye-catcher in every room. Concrete gives them stability.

HOW TO DO IT:
(1) If you use garden plant pots from a nursery, cover the pots with plastic wrap, and secure the plastic to the pots with rubber bands.
(2) Mix the concrete according to the package instructions, and pour into the pots. Insert the botanicals' stems, and wait for the concrete to dry. Then cut away the pots using scissors or garden clippers.

DRIED BOTANICALS:
· Sunflowers
· Giant hogweed
· Indian teasels
· Chinese silver grass

MATERIALS & TOOLS:
· Garden pots
· Quick-set concrete
· Bucket
· Wood stick for stirring
· Plastic wrap
· Rubber bands
· Scissors

WELCOME TO THE JUNGLE

Dressed up with a variety of dried botanicals, a natural wood plank can create a jungle feeling anywhere. Long branches placed casually against the wall will add texture.

HOW TO DO IT:
Attach a caged brick of dry-floral-foam, with tape, wire and/or hot glue, to the wood plank. Add some leaves sprayed with white paint. After drying, arrange the other dried botanicals into the dry-floral foam. Then simply lean the wood plank upright against the wall, or screw it to the wall for greater security.

DRIED BOTANICALS:
· Giant *Allium*
· *Tillandsia*
· Silver thistles/ Carline thistles
· Sago palm
· Chinese hemp palm
· Palmyra palm
· Pampas grass
· *Strelitzia* leaves

MATERIALS & TOOLS:
· Wood plank
· Caged dry-floral foam brick
· White spray paint
· Waterproof florist tape, wire and/or hot glue
· Scissors

77

WE LOVE
HANGING DÉCOR

Why should only lamps hang from the ceiling? Decorations with dried flowers can also be found here. Whether it's a flowery cloud, a maritime fishing net, a floating frieze or a gnarled branch sporting a tropical look, the following DIY hanging design ideas definitely offer something for everyone!

FLORAL SPHERE

Create this amazing design for a big party or just because you like it! This hanging botanical ball will make an impression anywhere it hangs! And creating it is surprisingly easy!

HOW TO DO IT:
It's so much easier to design with a dry-floral-foam sphere when it's suspended. Begin adding the flowers, and spin the design to see it come to life. Mix the materials well to create a coherent overall picture.

DRIED BOTANICALS:
· *Lunaria*
· Bleached butcher's broom
· *Eryngium*
· *Eucalyptus*
· Palmyra palm
· Pampas grass

MATERIALS & TOOLS:
· Extra-large dry-floral-foam sphere
· Tape
· Possibly a knife

81

HANGING TROPICALS

Who needs a vase when they have a gnarled branch? Hanging freely in a room, this innovative idea provides space for dried flowers and tropical plants such as ferns and palm leaves.

HOW TO DO IT:

The branch is drilled vertically in several places. Then wrap cord or paper-covered wire around the branch, near both ends, and hang the branch. Now, arrange the various botanicals into the drill holes. If desired, apply hot glue to the stem ends, for additional security.

DRIED BOTANICALS:
· *Hydrangea*
· *Protea*
· Purple-flowered *Allium*
· Silver wattle/Mimosa
· Wild teasels
· Sago palm
· Chinese hemp palm
· Palmyra palm
· Chinese silver grass

MATERIALS & TOOLS:
· Branch
· Cord or paper-covered wire
· Drill
· Possibly hot glue

83

WRAPPED ON WOOD

It doesn't always have to be wire. A wood hoop provides the perfect setting for this beautiful floral crescent of dried roses, ferns, cotton and other dried botanicals.

HOW TO DO IT:

Wire the botanical materials onto the wood hoop with binding wire until about a third of the hoop is covered. Design with florals thicker toward the middle and narrower toward the ends. Hang with twine or ribbon.

DRIED BOTANICALS:
· Australian immortelles
· Roses
· *Lunaria*
· *Eucalyptus*
· Balkan hogweed
· Barbed-wire plant
· Cotton
· Chinese silver grass
· Other ornamental grasses

MATERIALS & TOOLS:
· Wood hoop
· Twine or ribbon
· Binding wire

85

FLOATING FRIEZE

Whether you like this extra-large version or want something somewhat reduced in size, this floating frieze is guaranteed to elicit astonished looks from family and friends. Rabbit-cage wire serves as the basis.

HOW TO DO IT:
Cut the rabbit-cage wire (or chicken wire) to the desired length, and shape it into a long roll. Arrange the botanicals close together into the wire mesh structure. Hang the frieze with binding wire secured in several places.

DRIED BOTANICALS:
· *Hydrangea*
· Wild carrot
· Chinese silver grass
· Pampas grass

MATERIALS & TOOLS:
· Rabbit-cage wire or chicken wire
· Binding wire
· Wire cutters

MARITIME FISHING NET

Do you fancy an oceanside vacation? With fishing net, you can bring that aesthetic into a home! Perhaps you can even incorporate some of the shells from your last walk on the beach.

HOW TO DO IT:
(1) Cut about eight wool cords, each about 36 to 40 inches long, and knot them 2 or 3 inches apart onto a large branch. The total width of the cord structure should not exceed the length of the grass bundles. Attach string or twine to hang the design. Bundle the grasses, and weave the bundles horizontally through the hanging cords.
(2) So that nothing slips out, tie a knot with string or twine below each grass bundle. Drill holes into the shells, and wire them into the design. Add branches, ornamental onions and rapeseed throughout the design. Hot-glue paper fish into the design (clip art printed onto thick paper).

DRIED BOTANICALS:
· Ornamental onion
· Rapeseed
· Ornamental grasses
· Rustic branches or driftwood

MATERIALS & TOOLS:
· Seashells
· Paper fish
· Wool cord
· Binding wire
· Hot glue
· Drill
· Scissors

UPSIDE-DOWN FLOWERS

Dangling upside down from one or more wood beams, everlastings, opium poppies, billy buttons and other dried botanicals create a spectacular centerpiece above a table. Now the guests can come!

HOW TO DO IT:

(1) Drill two large holes, one at each end of a wood beam, and attach a suspension rope to the beam, through the holes. Knot the rope ends tightly and securely.
(2) Drill many smaller holes into the underside of the beam, and secure stems of various dried botanicals, as well as guinea fowl feathers, into the holes with hot glue.

DRIED BOTANICALS:
· Strawflowers
· Garden everlastings
· Opium poppies
· *Hydrangea*
· Billy buttons/
  Drumsticks
· Fennel
· Globe thistles
· Needle palm
· Palmyra palm
· Chinese silver grass

MATERIALS & TOOLS:
· Wood beam
· Guinea fowl feathers
· Rope
· Hot glue
· Drill
· Scissors

91

TWO
IN ONE

Bouquets or flower hoop? This piece of floral art combines both! Botanicals are bundled into tiny bouquets and attached to a metal ring, creating a dramatic statement design.

HOW TO DO IT:

(1) Bundle the grasses into small bunches, and wire them, upside down, onto a wire ring, spacing them about an inch or so apart. Leave about half of the ring free of material.
(2) Add the remaining botanical materials into the design with hot glue. You can also form small bunches and wire them into the design. Hang the design with twine or ribbon.

DRIED BOTANICALS:
· *Hydrangea*
· Statice/Sea lavender
· Strawflowers
· Immortelles
· *Lunaria*
· Chinese silver grass
· Spear grass

MATERIALS & TOOLS:
· Wire ring
· Binding wire
· Hot glue
· Twine or ribbon

AIRY SUMMER CLOUD

Dense shrubbery attached to a hanging branch looks like a floral cloud, with a variety of other dried botanicals wired in, to create an extravagantly decorative composition.

HOW TO DO IT:
Form the shrubbery into a cloud-like structure, and insert a long, narrow branch through it. Unwind some binding wire, crumple it, and place it into the shrubbery structure, attaching it to the branch. Arrange the stems of the other botanical materials into the shrubbery-and-crumpled-wire structure, and, if necessary, secure them with hot glue. Tie cord, twine or paper-covered wire to the ends of the branch to hang it.

DRIED BOTANICALS:
· *Hydrangea*
· Silver wattle/Mimosa
· Globe thistles
· *Eucalyptus*
· Needle palm
· Palmyra palm
· Sugar cane blooms
· Chinese silver grass
· Pampas grass
· Other ornamental
   grasses
· Shrubbery
· Long, narrow branch

MATERIALS
& TOOLS:
· Binding wire
· Cord, twine or
   paper-covered wire
· Possibly hot glue

95

CREDITS

PUBLISHER

WildFlower Media Inc.

With Permission BLOOM's GmbH

EDITING /TEXT

David Coake, WildFlower Media Inc.

Hella Henckel (vwtl.), Laura Marx, Karl-Michael Haake, BLOOM's GmbH

FLORAL DESIGNERS

Klaus Wagener, Team BLOOM's, Dany Eschenbüscher, Michael Sutmöller,

Petra Böttger, Sonja Deichmann, Dorothea Hamm, Anika Kuhlmann,

Doreen Neumann

PHOTOGRAPHY

BLOOM's GmbH/Alexander Heide, Patrick Pantze Images GmbH,

Except on the pages: 7 (Cally Lawson - pixabay.com), 9 (Petra Fischer - Fotolia.com, Annette

Meyer - pixabay.com), 10 (NKTN - shutterstock.com), 11 (NKTN - shutterstock.com, Annette

Meyer - pixabay.com, Hans Braxmeier - pixabay.com, Henryk Niestrój - pixabay.com), 12

(9c726_509 - istock.com), 14 (kalhh - pixabay.com)

GRAPHIC DESIGN

Kathleen Dillinger, Art Director

Mandy Schubert , Layout

U.S. Edition 2021
ISBN 978-1-7355603-5-9

Published in the United States
by WildFlower Media Inc.
© BLOOM's GmbH
https://Shop.WildFlower.Media

Wildflower.Media

Info@WildFlower.Media